The Christmas Angel

Abbie Farwell Brown

The Christmas Angel

Copyright © 2022 Indo-European Publishing

The present edition is a reproduction of previous publication of this classic work. Minor typographical errors may have been corrected without note; however, for an authentic reading experience the spelling, punctuation, and capitalization have been retained from the original text.

ISBN: 978-1-64439-887-6

CONTENTS

CONTENTS

CHAPTER I
THE PLAY BOX

At the sound of footsteps along the hall Miss Terry looked up from the letter which she was reading for the sixth time. "Of course I would not see him," she said, pursing her lips into a hard line. "Certainly not!"

A bump on the library door, as from an opposing knee, did duty for a knock.

"Bring the box in here, Norah," said Miss Terry, holding open the door for her servant, who was gasping under the weight of a packing-case. "Set it down on the rug by the fire-place. I am going to look it over and burn up the rubbish this evening."

She glanced once more at the letter in her hand, then with a sniff tossed it upon the fire.

"Yes'm," said Norah, as she set down the box with a thump. She stooped once more to pick up something which had fallen out when the cover was jarred open. It was a pink papier-mâché angel, such as are often hung from the top of Christmas trees as a crowning symbol. Norah stood holding it between thumb and finger, staring amazedly. Who would think to find such a bit of frivolity in the house of Miss Terry!

Her mistress looked up from the fire, where the bit of writing was writhing painfully, and caught the expression of Norah's face.

"What have you there?" she asked, frowning, as she took the

object into her own hands. "The Christmas Angel!" she exclaimed under her breath. "I had quite forgotten it." Then as if it burned her fingers she thrust the little image back into the box and turned to Norah brusquely. "There, that's all. You can go now, Norah," she said.

"Yes'm," answered the maid. She hesitated. "If you please'm, it's Christmas Eve."

"Well, I believe so," snapped Miss Terry, who seemed to be in a particularly bad humor this evening. "What do you want?"

Norah flushed; but she was hardened to her mistress's manner. "Only to ask if I may go out for a little while to see the decorations and hear the singing."

"Decorations? Singing? Fiddlestick!" retorted Miss Terry, poker in hand. "What decorations? What singing?"

"Why, all the windows along the street are full of candles," answered Norah; "rows of candles in every house, to light the Christ Child on his way when he comes through the city to-night."

"Fiddlestick!" again snarled her mistress.

"And choir-boys are going about the streets, they say, singing carols in front of the lighted houses," continued Norah enthusiastically. "It must sound so pretty!"

"They had much better be at home in bed. I believe people are losing their minds!"

"Please'm, may I go?" asked Norah again.

~ 2 ~

Norah had no puritanic traditions to her account. Moreover she was young and warm and enthusiastic. Sometimes the spell of Miss Terry's sombre house threatened her to the point of desperation. It was so this Christmas Eve; but she made her request with apparent calmness.

"Yes, go along," assented her mistress ungraciously.
"Thank you, 'm," said the servant demurely, but with a brightening of her blue eyes. And presently the area door banged behind her quick-retreating footsteps.

"H'm! Didn't take her long to get ready!" muttered Miss Terry, giving the fire a vicious poke. She was alone in the house, on Christmas Eve, and not a man, woman, or child in the world cared. Well, it was what she wanted. It was of her own doing. If she had wished—

She sat back in her chair, with thin, long hands lying along the arms of it, gazing into the fire. A bit of paper there was crumbling into ashes. Alone on Christmas Eve! Even Norah had some relation with the world outside. Was there not a stalwart officer waiting for her on the nearest corner? Even Norah could feel a simple childish pleasure in candles and carols and merriment, and the old, old superstition.

"Stuff and nonsense!" mused Miss Terry scornfully. "What is our Christmas, anyway? A time for shopkeepers to sell and for foolish folks to kill themselves in buying. Christmas spirit? No! It is all humbug,—all selfishness, and worry; an unwholesome season of unnatural activities. I am glad I am out of it. I am glad no one expects anything of me,—nor I of any one. I am quite independent; blessedly independent of the whole foolish business. It is a good time to begin clearing up for the new year. I'm glad I thought of it. I've long threatened to get rid of the stuff that has been accumulating in that corner of the attic. Now I will begin."

She tugged the packing-case an inch nearer the fire. It was like Miss Terry to insist upon that nearer inch. Then she raised the cover. It was a box full of children's battered toys, old-fashioned and quaint; the toys in vogue thirty—forty—fifty years earlier, when Miss Terry was a child. She gave a reminiscent sniff as she threw up the cover and saw on the under side of it a big label of pasteboard unevenly lettered.

PLAY BOX OF TOM TERRY AND ANGELINA TERRY
(scrawl)

"Humph!" she snorted. There was a great deal in that "humph." It meant: Yes, Tom's name had plenty of room, while poor little Angelina had to squeeze in as well as she could. How like Tom! This accounted for everything, even to his not being in his sister's house this very night. How unreasonable he had been!

Miss Terry shrugged impatiently. Why think of Tom to-night? Years ago he had deliberately cut himself adrift from her interests. No need to think of him now. It was too late to appease her. But here were all these toys to be got rid of. The fire was hungry for them. Why not begin?

Miss Terry stooped to poke over the contents of the box with lean, long fingers. In one corner thrust up a doll's arm; in another, an animal's tail pointed heavenward. She caught glimpses of glitter and tinsel, wheels and fragments of unidentifiable toys.

"What rubbish!" she said. "Yes, I'll burn them all. They are good

~ 4 ~

for nothing else. I suppose some folks would try to give them away, and bore a lot of people to death. They seem to think they are saving something, that way. Nonsense! I know better. It is all foolishness, this craze for giving. Most things are better destroyed as soon as you are done with them. Why, nobody wants such truck as this. Now, could any child ever have cared for so silly a thing?" She pulled out a faded jumping-jack, and regarded it scornfully. "Idiotic! Such toys are demoralizing for children—weaken their minds. It is a shame to think how every one seems bound to spoil children, especially at Christmas time. Well, no one can say that I have added to the shameful waste."

Miss Terry tossed the poor jumping-jack on the fire, and eyed his last contortions with grim satisfaction.

But as she watched, a quaint idea came to her. She was famous for eccentric ideas.

"I will try an experiment," she said. "I will prove once for all my point about the 'Christmas spirit.' I will drop some of these old toys out on the sidewalk and see what happens. It may be interesting."

CHAPTER II
JACK-IN-THE-BOX

Miss Terry rose and crossed two rooms to the front window, looking out upon the street. A flare of light almost blinded her eyes. Every window opposite her along the block, as far as she could see, was illuminated with a row of lighted candles across the sash. The soft, unusual glow threw into relief the pretty curtains and wreaths of green, and gave glimpses of cosy interiors and flitting happy figures.

"What a waste of candles!" scolded Miss Terry. "Folks are growing terribly extravagant."

The street was white with snow which had fallen a few hours earlier, piled in drifts along the curb of the little-traveled terrace. But the sidewalks were neatly shoveled and swept clean, as became the eminently respectable part of the city where Miss Terry lived. A long flight of steps, with iron railing at the side, led down from the front door, upon which a silver plate had for generations in decorous flourishes announced the name of Terry.

Miss Terry returned to the play box and drew out between thumb and finger the topmost toy. It happened to be a wooden box, with a wire hasp for fastening the cover. Half unconsciously she pressed the spring, and a hideous Jack-in-the-box sprang out to confront her with a squeak, a leering smile, and a red nose. Miss Terry eyed him with disfavor.

"I always did hate that thing," she said. "Tom was continually frightening me with it, I remember." As if to be rid of unwelcome memories she shut her mouth tight, even as she shut Jack back into his box, snapping the spring into place. "This will do to begin with," she thought. She crossed to the window, which she opened quickly, and tossed out the box, so that it fell squarely in the middle of the sidewalk. Then closing the window and turning down the lights in the room behind her, Miss Terry hid in the folds of the curtain and watched to see what would happen to Jack.

The street was quiet. Few persons passed on either side. At last she spied two little ragamuffins approaching. They seemed to be Jewish lads of the newsboy class, and they eyed the display of candles appraisingly. The smaller boy first caught sight of the box in the middle of the sidewalk.

"Hello! Wot's dis?" he grunted, making a dash upon it.
"Gee! Wot's up?" responded the other, who was instantly at his elbow.

"Gwan! Lemme look at it."

The smaller boy drew away and pressed the spring of the box eagerly. Ping! Out popped the Jack into his astonished face; whereupon he set up a guffaw.

"Give it here!" commanded the bigger boy.

"Naw! You let it alone! It's mine!" asserted the other, edging away along the curbstone. "I saw it first. You can't have it."

"Give it here. I saw it first myself. Hand it over, or I'll smash you!"

The bigger boy advanced threateningly.

"I won't!" the other whimpered, clasping the box tightly under his jacket.

He started to run, but the bigger fellow was too quick for him. He pounced across the sidewalk, and soon the twain were struggling in the snowdrift, pummeling one another with might and main.

"I told you so!" commented Miss Terry from behind the curtain. "Here's the first show of the beautiful Christmas spirit that is supposed to be abroad. Look at the little beasts fighting over something that neither of them really wants!"

Just then Miss Terry spied a blue-coated figure leisurely approaching. At the same moment an instinct seemed to warn the struggling urchins.

"Cop!" said a muffled voice from the pile of arms and legs, and in an instant two black shadows were flitting down the street; but not before the bigger boy had wrenched the box from the pocket of the little chap.

"So that is the end of experiment number one," quoth Miss Terry, smiling grimly. "It happened just about as I expected. They will be fighting again as soon as they are out of sight. They are Jews; but that doesn't make any difference about the Christmas spirit. Now let's see what becomes of the next experiment."

CHAPTER III
THE FLANTON DOG

She returned to the play box by the fire, and rummaged for a few minutes among the tangled toys. Then with something like a chuckle she drew out a soft, pale creature with four wobbly legs.

"The Flanton Dog!" she said. "Well, I vow! I had forgotten all about him. It was Tom who coined the name for him because he was made of Canton flannel."

She stood the thing up on the table as well as his weak legs would allow, and inspected him critically. He certainly was a forlorn specimen. One of the black beads which had served him for eyes was gone. His ears, which had originally stood up saucily on his head, now drooped in limp dejection. One of them was a mere shapeless rag hanging by a thread. He was dirty and discolored, and his tail was gone. But still he smiled with his red-thread mouth and seemed trying to make the best of things.

"What a nightmare!" said Miss Terry contemptuously. "I know there isn't a child in the city who wants such a looking thing. Why, even the Animal Rescue folks would give the boys a 'free shot' at that. This isn't going to bring out any Christmas spirit," she sneered. "I will try it and see."

Once more she lifted the window and tossed the dog to the sidewalk. He rolled upon his back and lay pathetically with crooked legs yearning upward, still smiling. Hardly had Miss

Terry time to conceal herself behind the curtain when she saw a figure approaching, airily waving a stick.

"No ragamuffin this time," she said. "Hello! It is that good-for-nothing young Cooper fellow from the next block. They say he is a millionaire. Well, he isn't even going to see the Flanton Dog."

The young man came swinging along, debonairly; he was whistling under his breath. He was a dapper figure in a long coat and a silk hat, under which the candles lighted a rather silly face. When he reached the spot in the sidewalk where the Flanton Dog lay, he paused a moment looking down. Then he poked the object with his stick. On the other side of the street a mother and her little boy were passing at the time. The child's eyes caught sight of the dog on the sidewalk, and he hung back, watching to see what the young man would do to it. But his mother drew him after her. Just then an automobile came panting through the snow. With a quick movement Cooper picked up the dog on the end of his stick and tossed it into the street, under the wheels of the machine. The baby across the street uttered a howl of anguish at the sight. Miss Terry herself was surprised to feel a pang shoot through her as the car passed over the queer old toy. She retreated from the window quickly.

"Well, that's the end of Flanton," she said with half a sigh. "I knew that fellow was a brute. I might have expected something like that. But it looked so—so—" She hesitated for a word, and did not finish her sentence, but bit her lip and sniffed cynically.

CHAPTER IV
THE NOAH'S ARK

"Now, what comes next?" Miss Terry rummaged in the box until her fingers met something odd-shaped, long, and smooth-sided. With some difficulty she drew out the object, for it was of good size.

"H'm! The old Noah's ark," she said. "I wonder if all the animals are in there."

She lifted the cover, and turned out into her lap the long-imprisoned animals and their round-bodied chief. Mrs. Noah and her sons had long since disappeared. But the ark-builder, hatless and one-armed, still presided over a menagerie of sorry beasts. Scarcely one could boast of being a quadruped. To few of them the years had spared a tail. From their close resemblance in their misery, it was not hard to believe in the kinship of all animal life. She took them up and examined them curiously one by one. Finally she selected a shapeless slate-colored block from the mass. "This was the elephant," she mused. "I remember when Tom stepped on him and smashed his trunk. 'I guess I'm going to be an expressman when I grow up,' he said, looking sorry. Tom was always full of his jokes. Now I'll try this and see what happens to the ark on its last voyage."

Just then there was a noise outside. An automobile honked past, and Miss Terry shuddered, recalling the pathetic end of the Flanton Dog, which had given her quite a turn.

"I hate those horrid machines!" she exclaimed. "They seem like

Juggernaut. I'd like to forbid their going through this street."

She crowded the elephant with Noah and the rest of his charge back into the ark and closed the lid. "I can't throw this out of the window," she reflected. "They would spill. I must take it out on the sidewalk. Land! The fire's going out! That girl doesn't know how to build fires so they will keep."

She laid the Noah's ark on the table, and going to the closet tugged out several big logs, which she arranged geometrically. About laying fires, as about most other things, Miss Terry had her own positive theories. Taking the bellows in hand she blew furiously, and was presently rewarded with a brisk blaze. She smiled with satisfaction, and trotted upstairs to find her red knit shawl. With this about her shoulders she was prepared to brave the December frost. Down the steps she went, and deposited the ark discreetly at their foot; then returned to take up her position behind the curtains.

There were a good many people passing, but they seemed too preoccupied to glance down at the sidewalk. They were nearly all hurrying in one direction. Some were running in the middle of the street.

"They are in a great hurry," sniffed Miss Terry disdainfully. "One would think they had something really important on hand. I suppose they are going to hear the singing. Fiddlestick!"

A man hastened by under the window; a woman; two children, a boy and a girl, running and gesticulating eagerly. None of them noticed the Noah's ark lying at the foot of the steps.

Miss Terry began to grow impatient. "Are they all blind?" she fretted. "What is the matter with them? I wish somebody would find the thing. I am tired of seeing it lying there."

She tapped the floor impatiently with her slipper. Just then a woman approached. She was dressed in the most uncompromising of mourning, and she walked slowly, with bent head, never glancing at the lighted windows on either side.

"She will see it," commented Miss Terry. And sure enough, she did. She stopped at the doorstep, drew her skirts aside, and bent over to look at the strange-shaped box at her feet. Finally she lifted it But immediately she shivered and acted so strangely that Miss Terry thought she was about to break the toy in pieces on the steps or throw it into the street. Evidently she detested the sight of it.

Just then up came a second woman with two small boys hanging at her skirts. They were ragged and sick-looking. There was something about the expression of even the tiny knot of hair at the back of the woman's head which told of anxious poverty. With envious curiosity she hurried up to see what a luckier mortal had found, crowding to look over her shoulder. The woman in black drew haughtily away and clutched the Noah's ark with a gesture of proprietorship.

"Go away! This is my affair." Miss Terry read her expression and sniffed. "There is the Christmas spirit coming out again," she said to herself. "Look at her face!"

The black-gowned woman prepared to move on with the toy under her arm. But the second woman caught hold of her skirt and began to speak earnestly. She pointed to the Noah's ark, then to her two children. Her eyes were beseeching. The little boys crowded forward eagerly. But some wicked spirit seemed to have seized the finder of the ark. Angrily she shook off the hand of the other woman, and clutching the box yet more firmly under her arm, she hurried away. Once, twice, she turned and shook her head at the ragged woman who followed her. Then, with a savage gesture at the two children, she disappeared beyond Miss Terry's straining eyes. The poor woman and her boys followed forlornly at a distance.

"They really wanted it, that old Noah's ark!" exclaimed Miss Terry in amazement. "I can scarcely believe it. But why did that other creature keep the thing? I see! Only because she found they cared for it. Well, that is a happy spirit for Christmas time, I should say! Humph! I did not expect to find anything quite so mean as that!"

CHAPTER V
MIRANDA

Miss Terry returned to the fireside, fumbled in the box, and drew out a doll. She was an ugly, old-fashioned doll, with bruised waxen face of no particular color. Her mop of flaxen hair was straggling and uneven, much the worse for the attention of generations of moths. She wore a faded green silk dress in the style of Lincoln's day, and a primitive bonnet, evidently made by childish hands. She was a strange, dead-looking figure, with pale eyelids closed, as Miss Terry dragged her from the box. But when she was set upright the lids snapped open and a pair of bright blue eyes looked straight into those of Miss Terry. It was so sudden that the lady nearly gasped.

"Miranda!" she exclaimed. "It is old Miranda! I have not thought of her for years." She held the doll at arm's length, gazing fixedly at her for some minutes.

"I cannot burn her," she muttered at last. "It would seem almost like murder. I don't like to throw her away, but I have vowed to get rid of these things to-night. And I'll do it, anyway. Yes, I'll make an experiment of her. I wonder what sort of trouble she will cause."

Not even Miss Terry could think of seeing old Miranda lying exposed to the winter night. She found a piece of paper, rolled up the doll in a neat package, and tied it with red string. It was, to look upon, entirely a tempting package. Once more she stole down the steps and hesitated where to leave Miranda: not on the sidewalk,—for some reason that seemed impossible. But

~ 15 ~

near the foot of the flight of steps leading to the front door she deposited the doll. The white package shone out plainly in the illuminated street. There was no doubt that it would be readily seen.

With a quite unexplainable interest Miss Terry watched to see what would happen to Miranda. She waited for some time. The street seemed deserted. Miss Terry caught the faint sound of singing. The choristers were passing through a neighboring street, and doubtless all wayfarers within hearing of their voices were following in their wake.

She was thoroughly interested in her grim joke, but she was becoming impatient. Were there to be no more passers? Must the doll stay there unreclaimed until morning? Presently she became aware of a child's figure drawing near. It was a little girl of about ten, very shabbily dressed, with tangled yellow curls hanging over her shoulders. There was something familiar about her appearance, Miss Terry could not say what it was. She came hurrying along the sidewalk with a preoccupied air, and seemed about to pass the steps without seeing the package lying there. But just as she was opposite the window, her eye caught the gleam of the white paper. She paused. She looked at it eagerly; it was such a tempting package, both as to its size and shape! She went closer and bent down to examine it. She took it into her bare little hands and seemed to squeeze it gently. There is no mistaking the contours of a doll, however well it may be enveloped in paper wrappings. The child's eyes grew more and more eager. She glanced behind her furtively; she looked up and down the street. Then with a sudden intuition she looked straight ahead, up the flight of steps.

Miss Terry read her mind accurately. She was thinking that probably the doll belonged in that house; some one must have dropped the package while going out or in. Would she ring the bell and return it? Miss Terry had not thought of that possibility. But she shook her head and her lip curled. "Return it? Of course not! Ragged children do not usually return promising packages which they have found,—even on Christmas Eve. Look now!"

Once more the child glanced stealthily behind her, up and down the street. Once more she looked up at the dark house before her, the only black spot in a wreath of brilliancy. She did not see the face peering at her through the curtains, a face which scanned her own half wistfully. What was to become of Miranda? The little girl thrust the package under her ragged coat and ran away down the street as fast as her legs could take her.

"A thief!" cried Miss Terry. "That is the climax. I have detected a child taking what she knew did not belong to her, on Christmas Eve! Where are all their Sunday School lessons and their social improvement classes? I knew it! This Christmas spirit that one hears so much about is nothing but an empty sham. I have proved it to my satisfaction to-night. I will burn the rest of these toys, every one of them, and then go to bed. It is too disgusting! She was a nice-looking child, too. Poor old Miranda!"

With something like a sigh Miss Terry strode back to the fire, where the play box stood gaping. She had made but a small inroad upon its heaped-up treasures. She threw herself listlessly into the chair and began to pull over the things. Broken games and animals, dolls' dresses painfully tailored by unskilled fingers, disjointed members,—sorry relics of past pleasures,—one by one Miss Terry seized them between disdainful thumb and finger and tossed them into the fire. Her face showed not a qualm at parting with these childhood treasures; only the stern sense of a good housekeeper's duty fulfilled. With queer contortions the bits writhed on the coals, and finally flared into dissolution, vanishing up chimney in a shower of sparks to the heaven of spent toys.

CHAPTER VI
THE CHRISTMAS ANGEL

Almost at the bottom of the box Miss Terry's fingers closed about a small object. Once more she drew out the papier-mâché Angel which had so excited the wonder of Norah when once before that evening it had come to light.

Miss Terry held it up and looked at it with the same expression on her face, half tender, half contemptuous. "The Christmas Angel!" she murmured involuntarily, as she had done before. And again there flashed through her mind a vivid picture.

It was the day before Christmas, fifty years earlier. She and her brother Tom were trimming the Christmas tree in this very library. She saw Tom, in a white piqué suit with short socks that were always slipping down his fat legs. She saw herself in a white dress and blue ribbons, pouting in a corner. They had been quarreling about the Christmas tree, disputing as to which of them should light the first candle when the time arrived. Then their mother came to them smiling, a sweet-faced lady who seemed not to notice the red faces and the tears. She put something into Tom's hand saying, "This is the Christmas Angel of peace and good-will. Hang it on the tree, children, so that it may shed a blessing on all who come here to give and to receive."

How lovely and pink it looked in Tom's hand! Little Angelina had thought it the most beautiful thing she had ever seen,— and holy, too, as if it had some blessed charm. Fiddlestick! What queer fancies children have! Miss Terry remembered how a strange thrill had crept through Angelina as she gazed at it. Then she and Tom looked at each other and were ashamed of their quarrel. Suddenly Tom held out the Angel to his sister. "You hang it on the tree, Angelina," he said magnanimously. "I know you want to."

But she—little fool!—she too had a fit of generosity.

"No, you hang it, Tom. You're taller," she said.

"I'll hang it at the very top of the tree!" he replied, nothing loath. Eagerly he mounted the step-ladder, while Angelina watched him enviously, thinking how clumsy he was, and how much better she could do it.

How funny and fat Tom had looked on top of the ladder, reaching as high as he dared! The ladder began to wobble, and he balanced precariously, while Angelina clutched at his fat ankles with a scream of fright. But Tom said:—

"Ow! Angelina, let go my ankles! You hurt! Now don't scream. I shan't fall. Don't you know that this is the Christmas Angel, and he will never let me get hurt on Christmas Eve?"

Swaying wildly on one toe Tom had clutched at the air, at the tree itself,—anywhere for support. Yet, almost as if by a miracle, he did not fall. And the Christmas Angel was looking down from the very top of the tree.

Miss Terry laid the little pink figure in her lap and mused. "Mother was wise!" she sighed. "She knew how to settle our quarrels in those days. Perhaps if she had still been here things would have gone differently. Tom might not have left me for good. For good." She emphasized the words with a nod as if arguing against something.

Again she took up the Christmas Angel and looked earnestly at it. Could it be that tears were glistening in her eyes? Certainly not! With a sudden sniff and jerk of the shoulders she leaned forward, holding the Angel towards the fire. This should follow the other useless toys. But something seemed to stay her hand. She drew back, hesitated, then rose to her feet.

"I can't burn it," she said. "It's no use, I can't burn it. But I don't want to see the thing around. I will put this out on the sidewalk, too. Possibly this may be different and do some good to somebody."

She wrapped the shawl about her shoulders and once more ran down the steps. She left the Angel face upward in the middle of the sidewalk, and retreated quickly to the house. As she opened the door to enter, she caught the distant chorus of fresh young voices singing in a neighboring square:—
"Angels from the realms of glory, Wing your flight o'er all the earth."

When she took her place behind the curtain she was trembling a little, she could not guess why. But now she watched with renewed eagerness. What was to be the fate of the Christmas Angel? Would he fall into the right hands and be hung upon some Christmas tree ere morning? Would he—

Miss Terry held her breath. A man was staggering along the street toward her. He whistled noisily a vulgar song, as he reeled from curb to railing, threatening to fall at every step. A drunken man on Christmas Eve! Miss Terry felt a great loathing for him. He was at the foot of the steps now. He was close upon the Angel. Would he see it, or would he tread upon it in his disgusting blindness?

Yes—no! He saw the little pink image lying on the bricks, and with a lurch forward bent to examine it. Miss Terry flattened her nose against the pane eagerly. She expected to see him fall upon the Angel bodily. But no; he righted himself with a whoop of drunken mirth.

"Angel!" she heard him croak with maudlin accent. "Pink Angel, begorrah! What doin' 'ere, eh? Whoop! Go back to sky, Angel!" and lifting a brutal foot he kicked the image into the street. Then with a shriek of laughter he staggered away out of sight.

Miss Terry found herself trembling with indignation. The idea! He had kicked the Christmas Angel,—the very Angel that Tom had hung on their tree! It was sacrilege, or at least—Fiddlestick! Miss Terry's mind was growing confused. She had a sudden impulse to rescue the toy from being trampled into filthiness. The fire was better than that.

She hurried down the steps into the street, forgetting her shawl. She sought in the snow and snatched the pink morsel to safety. Straight to the fire she carried it, and once more held it to the flames. But again she found it impossible to burn the thing. Once, twice, she tried. But each time something seemed to clutch back her wrist. At last she shrugged impatiently and laid the Angel on the mantelpiece beside the square old marble clock, which marked the hour of half-past eight.

"Well, I won't burn it to-night," she reflected. "Somehow, I can't do it just now. I don't see what has got into me! But to-morrow I will. Yes, to-morrow I will."

She sat down in the armchair and fumbled in the old play box for the remaining scraps. There were but a few meaningless bits of ribbon and gauze, with the end of a Christmas candle, the survivor of some past festival, burned on some tree in the past. All these but the last she tossed into the fire, where they made a final protesting blaze. The candle-end fell to the floor unnoticed.

"There! That is the last of the stuff," she exclaimed with grim satisfaction, shaking the dust from her black silk skirt. "It is all gone now, thank Heaven, and I can go to bed in peace. No, I forgot Norah. I suppose I must sit up and wait for her. Bother the girl! She ought to be in by now. What can she find to amuse her all this time? Christmas Eve! Fiddlestick! But I have got rid of a lot of rubbish to-night, and that is worth something."

She sank back in her chair and clasped her hands over her breast with a sigh. She felt strangely weary. Her eyes sought the clock once more, and doing so rested upon the Christmas Angel lying beside it. She frowned and closed her eyes to shut out the sight with its haunting memories and suggestions— —

CHAPTER VII
BEFORE THE FIRE

Suddenly there was a volume of sound outside, and a great brightness filled the room. Miss Terry opened her eyes. The fire was burning red; but a yellow light, as from thousands of candles, shone in at the window, and there was the sound of singing, — the sweetest singing that Miss Terry had ever heard. "An Angel of the Lord came down, And glory shone around."

The words seemed chanted by the voices of young angels. Miss Terry passed her hands over her eyes and glanced at the clock. But what the hour was she never noticed, for her gaze was filled with something else. Beside the clock, in the spot where she had laid it a few minutes before, was the Christmas Angel. But now, instead of lying helplessly on its back, it was standing on rosy feet, with arms outstretched toward her. Over its head fluttered gauzy wings. From under the yellow hair which rippled over the shoulders two blue eyes beamed kindly upon her, and the mouth widened into the sweetest smile.
"Peace on earth to men of good-will!" cried the Angel, and the tone of his speech was music, yet quite natural and thrilling.

Miss Terry stared hard at the Angel and rubbed her eyes, saying to herself, "Fiddlestick! I am dreaming!"

But she could not rub away the vision. When she opened her eyes the Angel still stood tiptoe on the mantel-shelf, smiling at her and shaking his golden head.

"Angelina!" said the Angel softly; and Miss Terry trembled to hear her name thus spoken for the first time in years. "Angelina, you do not want to believe your own eyes, do you? But I am real; more real than the things you see every day. You must believe in me. I am the Christmas Angel."

"I know it." Miss Terry's voice was hoarse and unmanageable, as of one in a nightmare. "I remember."

"You remember!" repeated the Angel. "Yes; you remember the day when you and Tom hung me on the Christmas tree. You were a sweet little girl then, with blue eyes and yellow curls. You believed the Christmas story and loved Santa Claus. Then you were simple and affectionate and generous and happy."

"Fiddlestick!" Miss Terry tried to say. But the word would not come.

"Now you have lost the old belief and the old love," went on the Angel. "Now you have studied books and read wise men's sayings. You understand the higher criticism, and the higher charity, and the higher egoism. You don't believe in mere giving. You don't believe in the Christmas economics,—you know better. But are you happy, dear Angelina?"

Again Miss Terry thrilled at the sound of her name so sweetly spoken; but she answered nothing. The Angel replied for her.

"No, you are not happy because you have cut yourself off from the things that bring folk together in peace and good-will at this holy time. Where are your friends? Where is your brother to-night? You are still hard and unforgiving to Tom. You refused to see him to-day, though he wrote so boyishly, so humbly and affectionately. You have not tried to make any soul happy. You don't believe in me, the Christmas Spirit."

There is such a word as Fiddlestick, whatever it may mean. But Miss Terry's mind and tongue were unable to form it.

"The Christmas spirit!" continued the Angel. "What is life worth if one cannot believe in the Christmas spirit?"

With a powerful effort Miss Terry shook off her nightmare sufficiently to say, "The Christmas spirit is no real thing. I have proved it to-night. It is not real. It is a humbug!"

"Not real? A humbug?" repeated the Angel softly. "And you have proved it, Angelina, this very night?"

Miss Terry nodded.

"I know what you have done," said the Angel. "I know very well. How keen you were! How clever! You made a test of Chance, to prove your point."

Again Miss Terry nodded with complacency.

"What knowledge of the world! What grasp of human nature!" commented the Angel, smiling. "It is like you mere mortals to say, 'I will make my test in my own way. If certain things happen, I shall foresee what the result must be. If certain other things happen, I shall know that I am right.' Events fall out as you expect, and you smile with satisfaction, feeling your wisdom justified. It ought to make you happy. But does it?"

Miss Terry regarded the Angel doubtfully.

"Look now!" he went on, holding up a rosy finger. "You are so near-sighted! You are so unimaginative! You do not dream beyond the thing you see. You judge the tale finished while the best has yet to be told. And you stake your faith, your hope, your charity upon this blind human judgment,—which is mere Chance!"

Miss Terry opened her lips to say, "I saw—" but the Angel interrupted her.

"You saw but the beginning," he said. "You saw but the first page of each history. Shall I turn over the leaves and let you read what really happened? Shall I help you to see the whole truth instead of a part? On this night holy Truth, which is of Heaven, comes for all men to see and to believe. Look!"

CHAPTER VIII
JACK AGAIN

The Christmas Angel gently waved his hand to and fro. Gradually, as Miss Terry sat back in her chair, the library grew dark; or rather, things faded into an indistinguishable blur. Then it seemed as if she were sitting at a theatre gazing at a great stage. But at this theatre there was nothing about her, nothing between her and the place where things were happening.

First she saw two little ragamuffins quarreling over something in the snow. She recognized them. They were the two Jewish boys who had picked up the Jack-in-the-box. An officer appeared, and they ran away, the bigger boy having possession of the toy; the smaller one with fists in his eyes, bawling with disappointment.

Miss Terry's lips curled with the cynical disgust which she had felt when first witnessing this scene. But a sweet voice—and she knew it was the Angel's—whispered in her ear, "Wait and see!"

She watched the two boys run through the streets until they came to a dark corner. There the little fellow caught up with the other, and once more the struggle began. It was a hard and bloody fight. But this time the victory was with the smaller lad, who used his fists and feet like an enraged animal, until the other howled for mercy and handed over the disputed toy.

"Whatcher want it fer, Sam?" he blubbered as he saw it go into the little fellow's pocket.

"Mind yer own business! I just want it," answered Sam surlily.

"Betcher I know," taunted the bigger boy.

"Betcher yer don't."

"Do!"

"Don't!"

Another fight seemed imminent. But wisdom prevailed with Sammy. He would not challenge fate a third time. "Come on, then, and see," he grunted.

And Ike followed. Off the two trudged, through the brilliantly lighted streets, until they came to a part of the city where the ways were narrower and dark.
"Huh! Knowed you was comin' here," commented Ike as they turned into a grim, dirty alley.

Little Sam growled, "Didn't!" apparently as a matter of habit.

"Did!" reasserted Ike. "Just where I was comin' myself."

Sam turned to him with a grin.

"Was yer now? By—! Ain't that funny? I thought of it right off."

"Sure. Same here!"

They both burst into a guffaw and executed an impromptu double-shuffle of delight. They were at the door of a tenement house with steep stairs leading into darkness. Up three flights pounded the two pairs of heavy boots, till they reached a half-open door, whence issued the clatter of a sewing-machine and the voices of children. Sam stood on the threshold grinning debonairly, with hands thrust into his pockets. Ike peered over his shoulder, also grinning.

It was a meagre room into which they gazed, a room the chief furniture of which seemed to be babies. Two little ones sprawled on the floor. A third tiny tot lay in a broken-down carriage beside the door. A pale, ill-looking woman was running the machine. On the cot bed was crumpled a fragile little fellow of about five, and a small pair of crutches lay across the foot of the bed.

When the two boys appeared in the doorway, the woman stopped her machine and the children set up a howl of pleasure. "Sammy! Ikey!" cried the woman, smiling a wan welcome, as the babies crept and toddled toward the newcomers. "Where ye come from?"

"Been to see the shops and the lights in the swell houses," answered Sammy with a grimace. "Gee! Ain't they wastin' candles to beat the cars!"

"Enough to last a family a whole year," muttered Ike with disgust.

The woman sighed. "Maybe they ain't wasted exactly," she said. "How I'd like to see 'em! But I got to finish this job. I told the chil'ren they mustn't expect anything this Christmas. But they are too little to know the difference anyway; all but Joe. I wish I had something for Joe."

"I got something for Joe," said Sammy unexpectedly.
The face of the pale little cripple lighted.

"What is it?" he asked eagerly. "Oh, what is it? A real Christmas present for me?"

"Naw! It ain't a Christmas present," said Sam.

"We don't care anything about Christmas," volunteered Ikey with a grin.

Sam looked at him with a frown of rebuke.

"It's just a present," he said. "And it didn't cost a cent. I didn't buy it. I—we found it!"

"Found it in the street?" Joe's eyes shone.

"Yah!" the boys nodded.

"Oh, it is a Christmas present!" cried Joe. "Santa Claus must have dropped it there for me, because he knew we hadn't any chimney in this house, and he sent you kind, kind boys to bring it to me."

The two urchins looked sideways at each other, but said nothing. Presently Sam drew out the box from his pocket and tried to thrust it into Ike's hand. "You give it to 'um," he said. "You're the biggest."

"Naw! You give it. You found it," protested Ike.
"Ah, g'wan!"

"Big fool!"

There was a tussle, and it almost seemed as if the past unpleasantness was to be repeated from an opposite cause. But Joe's voice settled the dispute.

"Oh, Sammy, please!" he cried. "I can't wait another minute. Do please give it to me now!"

At these words Sam stepped forward without further argument and laid the box on the bed in front of the little cripple. The babies crowded about. The mother left her machine and stood smiling faintly at the foot of the bed.

Joe pressed the spring. Ping! Out sprang the Jack-in-the-box, with the same red nose, the same leer, the same roguish eyes which had surprised the children of fifty years ago.

Jack was always sure of his audience. My! How they screamed and begged Joe to "do it again." And as for Joe, he lay back on his pillow and laughed and laughed as though he would never stop. It was the first Jack any of them had seen.

Tears stood in the mother's eyes. "Well," she said, "it's as good as a play to see him. Joe hasn't laughed like that for months. You boys have done him lots of good. I wouldn't wonder if it helped him get well! If you was Christians I'd say you showed the real Christmas spirit. But Lord—perhaps ye do, all the same! I dunno!"

Sam and Ike were so busy playing with the children that they did not hear.

Gradually the tenement house faded and became a blur before Miss Terry's eyes. Once more she saw the mantel-shelf before her and the Christmas Angel with outstretched arms waving to and fro. "You see!" he said. "You did not guess all the pleasure that was shut up in that box with old Jack, did you?"

Miss Terry shook her head.

"And you see how different it all was from what you thought. Now let us see what became of the Canton-flannel dog."

"The Flanton Dog." Miss Terry amended the phrase under her breath. It seemed so natural to use Tom's word.

"Yes, the Flanton Dog," the Angel smiled. "What do you think became of him?"
"I saw what became of him," said Miss Terry. "Bob Cooper threw him under an automobile, and he was crushed flatter than a pancake."

"Then you left the window," said the Angel. "In your human way you assumed that this was the end. But wait and see."

Once more the room darkened and blurred, and Miss Terry looked out upon past events as upon a busy, ever-shifting stage.

CHAPTER IX
THE DOG AGAIN

She saw the snowy street, into which, from the tip of his stick, Bob Cooper had just tossed the Flanton Dog. She saw, what she had not seen before, the woman and child on the opposite side of the street. She saw the baby stretch out wistful hands after the dog lying in the snow. Then an automobile honked past, and she felt again the thrill of horror as it ran over the poor old toy. At the same moment the child screamed, and she saw it point tearfully at the Flanton tragedy. The mother, who had seen nothing of all this, stooped and spoke to him reprovingly.

"What's the matter, Johnnie?" she said. "Sh! Don't make such a noise. Here we are at Mrs. Wales's gate, and you mustn't make a fuss. Now be a good boy and wait here till Mother comes out."

She rang the area bell and stood basket in hand, waiting to be admitted. But Johnnie gazed at one spot in the street, with eyes full of tears, and with now and then a sob gurgling from his throat. He could not forget what he had seen.

The door opened for the mother, who disappeared inside the house, with one last command to the child: "Now be a good boy, Johnnie. I'll be back in half a minute."

Hardly was she out of sight when Johnnie started through the snowdrift toward the middle of the street. With difficulty he lifted his little legs out of the deep snow; now and then he stumbled and fell into the soft mass. But he rose only the more determined upon his errand, and kept his eyes fixed on the wreck of the Flanton Dog.

Bob Cooper, who was idly strolling up and down the block, smoking a cigarette, as he watched the flitting girlish shadows in a certain window opposite, saw the child's frantic struggles in the snow and was intensely amused. "Bah Jove!" he chuckled. "I believe he's after the wretched dawg that I tossed over there with my stick. Fahncy it!" And carelessly he puffed a whiff of smoke.

At last the baby reached the middle of the street and stooped to pick up the battered toy. It was flattened and shapeless, but the child clasped it tenderly and began to coo softly to it.

"Bah Jove!" repeated Cooper. "Fahncy caring so much about anything! Poor kid! Perhaps that is all the Christmas he will have." He blew a thoughtful puff through his nose. "Christmas Eve!" The thought flashed through his mind with a new appeal.

Just then came a sudden "Honk, honk!" An automobile had turned the corner and was coming up at full speed. It was the same machine which had passed a few minutes earlier in the opposite direction.

"Hi there!" Cooper yelled to the child. But the latter was sitting in the snow in the middle of the street, rocking back and forth, with the Flanton Dog in his arms. There was scarcely time for action. Bob dropped his cigarette and his cane, made one leap into the street and another to the child, and by the impact of his body threw the baby into the drift at the curb. With a horrified honk the automobile passed over the young man, who lay senseless in the snow.

He was not killed. Miss Terry saw him taken to his home close by, where his broken leg was set and his bruises attended to. She saw him lying bandaged and white on his bed when the woman and her child were brought to see him. Johnnie was still clasping closely the unlucky Flanton Dog.

"Well, Kid," said the young man feebly, "so you saved the dog, after all."
"O sir!" cried the poor woman, weeping. "Only to think that he would not be here now but for you. What a Christmas that would have been for me! You were so good, so brave!"

"Oh, rot!" protested Bob faintly. "Had to do it; my fault anyway; Christmas Eve,—couldn't see a kid hurt on Christmas Eve."

He called the attendant and asked for the pocket-book which had been in his coat at the time of the accident. Putting it into the woman's hand, he said, "Good-by. Get Johnnie something really jolly for Christmas. I'm afraid the dog is about all in. Get him a new one."

But Johnnie refused to have a new dog. It was the poor, shapeless Flanton animal which remained the darling of his heart for many a moon.

All this of past and future Miss Terry knew through the Angel's power. When once more the library lightened, and she saw the pink figure smiling at her from the mantel, she spoke of her own accord.

"It was my fault, because I put the dog in the way. I caused all that trouble."

"Trouble?" said the Angel, puzzled. "Do you call it trouble? Do you not see what it has done for that heartless youth? It brought his good moment. Perhaps he will be a different man after this. And as for the child; he was made happy by something that would otherwise have been wasted, and he has gained a friend who will not forget him. Trouble! And do you think you did it?" He laughed knowingly.

"I certainly did," said Miss Terry firmly.

"But it was I, yes I, the Christmas Spirit, who put it into your head to do what you did. You may not believe it, but so it was. You too, even you, Angelina, could not quite escape the influence of the Christmas Spirit, and so these things have happened. But now let us see what became of the third experiment."

CHAPTER X
NOAH AGAIN

In the street of candles a woman dressed all in black had picked up the poor old Noah's ark and was looking at it wildly. She was a widow who had just lost her only child, a little son, and she was in a state of morbid bitterness bordering on distraction.

When the second woman with the two little ones came up and begged for the toy, something hard and sullen and cruel rose in the widow's heart, and she refused angrily to give up the thing. She hated those two boys who had been spared when her own was taken. She would not make them happy.

"No, you shall not have it," she cried, clutching the Noah's ark fiercely. "I will destroy it."

The poor woman and the children followed her wistfully. The little boys were crying. They were cold and hungry and disappointed. They had come so near to something pleasant. They had almost been lucky; but the luck had passed over their heads to another.

The woman in mourning strode on rapidly, the thoughts within her no less black than the garments which she wore. She hated the world; she hated the people who lived in it. She hated Christmas time, when every one seemed merry except herself. And yes, yes! Most of all she hated children. She clenched her teeth wickedly; her mind reeled.

Suddenly, somewhere, a chorus of happy voices began to sing the words of an old carol:—
"Holy night! Peaceful night! All is dark save the light, Yonder where they sweet vigil keep, O'er the Babe who in silent sleep Rests in heavenly peace."

Softly and sweetly the childish voices ascended from the street. The woman in black stopped short, breathing hard. She saw the band of choristers standing in a group on the sidewalk and in the snow, their hats pulled down over their eyes, their collars turned up around their ears, their hands deep in pockets. In their midst rose the tall wooden cross carried by a little fellow with yellow hair. They sang as simply and as heartily as a flock of birds out in the snow.

The woman gave a great sob. Her little lad had been a choir boy,—perhaps these were his one-time comrades. The second verse of the carol rang out sweetly:—
"Holy night! Peaceful night! Only for shepherds' sight Came blest visions of angel throngs, With their loud Hallelujah songs, Saying, Jesus is come!"

Suddenly it seemed to the distracted mother that her own boy's voice blended with those others. He too was singing in honor of that Child. Happy and ever young, he was bidding her rejoice in the day which made all childhood sacred. And for his sake she had been hating children!

With a sudden revulsion of feeling she turned to see what had become of the poor mother and her boys. They were not far behind, huddling in the shadow. The black woman strode quickly up to them. They shrank pitifully at her approach, and she felt the shame of it. They were afraid of her!

"Here," she said, thrusting the Noah's ark into the hands of the larger boy. "Take it. It belongs to you."

The child took it timidly. The mother began to protest thanks. Trying to control the shake in her voice the dark lady spoke again. "Have you prepared a Christmas for your children?"

The woman shook her head. "I have nothing," she sighed. "A roof over our heads, that's all."

"Your husband?"

"My man died a month ago."

So other folk had raw sorrows, too. The mourner had forgotten that.

"There is no one expecting you at home?" Again the woman shook her head dolefully. "Come with me," said the dark lady impulsively. "You shall be my guests to-night. And to-morrow I will make a Christmas for the children. The house shall put off its shadow. I too will light candles. I have toys,"—her voice broke,—"and clothing; many things, which are being wasted. That is not right! Something led you to me, or me to you; something,—perhaps it was an Angel,—whoever dropped that Noah's ark in the street. An Angel might do that, I believe. Come with me."

The woman and her sons followed her, rejoicing greatly in the midst of their wonder.

There were tears in the eyes through which Miss Terry saw once more the Christmas Angel. She wiped them hastily. But still the Angel seemed to shine with a fairer radiance.

"You see!" was all he said. And Miss Terry bowed her head. She began to understand.

CHAPTER XI
MIRANDA AGAIN

Once more, on the wings of vision, Miss Terry was out in the snowy street. She was following the fleet steps of a little girl who carried a white-paper package under her arm. Miss Terry knew that she was learning the fate of her old doll, Miranda, whom her own hands had thrust out into a cold world.

Poor Miranda! After all these years to become the property of a thief! Mary was the little thief's name. Hugging the tempting package close, Mary ran and ran until she was out of breath. Her one thought was to get as far as possible from the place where the bundle had lain. For she suspected that the steps where she had found it led up to the doll's home. That was why in her own eyes also she was a little thief. But now she had run so far and had turned so many corners that she could not find her way back if she would. There was triumph in the thought. Mary chuckled to herself as she stopped running and began to walk leisurely in the neighborhood with which she was more familiar.

She pinched the package gently. Yes, there could be no doubt about it. It was a doll,—not a very large doll; but Mary reflected that she had never thought she should care for a large doll. Undoubtedly it was a very nice one. Had she not found it in a swell part of the city, on the steps of a swell-looking house? Mary gloated over the doll as she fancied it; with real hair, and eyes that opened and shut; with four little white teeth, and hands with dimples in the knuckles. She had seen such dolls in the windows of the big shops. But she had never hoped to have one for her very own.

"Maybe it will have on a blue silk dress and white kid shoes, like that one I saw this morning!" she mused rapturously.

She pinched the spot where she fancied the doll's feet ought to be.

"Yes, she's got shoes, sure enough! I bet they're white, too. They feel white. Oh, what fun I shall have with her,"—she hugged the doll fondly,—"if Uncle and Aunt don't take her away!"

The sudden thought made her stand still in horror. "They sold Mother's little clock for rum," she said bitterly. "They sold the ring with the red stone that Father gave me on my birthday when I was seven. They sold the presents that I got at Sunday School last year. Oh, wouldn't it be dreadful if they should sell my new doll! And I know they will want to if they see her." She squeezed the bundle closer with the prescient pang of parting.

"Maybe they'll be out somewhere." With this faint hope she reached the tenement and crept up the dingy stairs. She peeped in at the door. Alas! Her uncle and aunt were in the kitchen, through which she had to pass. They had company; some dirty-looking men and women, and there were a jug and glasses on the table before them. Mary's heart sank, but she nodded bravely to the company and tried to slip through the crowd to the other room. But her aunt was quick to see that she carried something under her coat.

"What you got there? A Christmas present?" she sneered.

Mary flushed. "No," she said slowly, "just something I found."

"Found? Hello, what is it? A package!"

Her uncle advanced and snatched it from her.

"Please," pleaded Mary, "please, I found it. It is mine. I think it is only a doll."

"A doll! Huh! Who needs a doll?" hiccoughed her uncle. "We want something more to drink. We'll sell it—"

A bellow of laughter resounded through the room. The paper being torn roughly away, poor Miranda stood revealed in all her faded beauty. The pallid waxen face, straggling hair, and old-fashioned dress presented a sorry sight to the greedy eyes which had expected to find something exchangeable for drink. A sorry sight she was to Mary, who had hoped for something so much lovelier. A flush of disappointment came into her cheek, and tears to her eyes.

"Here, take your old doll," said her uncle roughly, thrusting it into her arms. "Take your old doll and get away with her. If that's the best you can find you'd better steal something next time."

Steal something! Had she not in fact stolen it? Mary knew very well that she had, and she flushed pinker yet to think what a fool she had made of herself for nothing. She took the despised doll and retreated into the other room, followed by a chorus of jeers and comments. She banged the door behind her and sat down with poor Miranda on her knees, crying as if her heart would break. She had so longed for a beautiful doll! It did seem too cruel that when she found one it should turn out to be so ugly. She seized poor Miranda and shook her fiercely.

"You horrid old thing!" she said. "Ain't you ashamed to fool me so? Ain't you ashamed to make me think you was a lovely doll with pretty clo'es and white kid shoes? Ain't you?"

She shook Miranda again until her eyeballs rattled in her head.

The doll fell to the floor and lay there with closed eyes. Her face was pallid and ghastly. Her bonnet had fallen off, and her hair stuck out wildly in every direction. Her legs were doubled under her in the most helpless fashion. She was the forlornest figure of a doll imaginable. Presently Mary drew her hands away from her eyes and looked down at Miranda. There was something in the doll's attitude as she lay there which touched the little girl's heart. Once she had seen a woman who had been injured in the street,—she would never forget it. The poor creature's eyes had been closed, and her face, under the fallen bonnet, was of this same pasty color. Mary shuddered. Suddenly she felt a warm rush of pity for the doll.

"You poor old thing!" she exclaimed, looking at Miranda almost tenderly. "I'm sorry I shook you. You look so tired and sad and homesick! I wonder if somebody is worrying about you this minute. It was very wicked of me to take you away— on Christmas Eve, too! I wish I had left you where I found you. Maybe some little girl is crying now because you are lost."

Mary stooped and lifted the doll gently upon her knees. As she took Miranda up, the blue eyes opened and seemed to look full at her. Miranda's one beauty was her eyes. Mary felt her heart grow warmer and warmer toward the quaint stranger.

"You have lovely eyes," she murmured. "I think after all you are almost pretty. Perhaps I should grow to like you awfully. You are not a bit like the doll I hoped to have; but that is not your fault." A thought made her face brighten. "Why, if you had been a beautiful doll they would have taken you away and sold you for rum." Her face expressed utter disgust. She hugged Miranda close with a sudden outburst of affection. "Oh, you dear old thing!" she cried. "I am so glad you are—just like this. I am so glad, for now I can keep you always and always, and no one will want to take you away from me."

She rocked to and fro, holding the doll tightly to her heart. Mary was not one to feel a half-passion about anything. "I will make you some new dresses," she said, fingering the old-fashioned silk with a puzzled air. "I wonder why your mother dressed you so queerly? She was not much of a sewer if she made this bonnet!" Scornfully she took off the primitive bonnet and smoothed out the tangled hair. "I wonder what you have on underneath," she said.

With gentle fingers she began to undress Miranda. Off came the green silk dress with its tight "basque" and overskirt. Off came the ruffled petticoat and little chemise edged with fine lace. And Miranda stood in shapeless, kid-bodied ugliness, which stage of evolution the doll of her day had reached.

But there was something more. Around her neck she wore a ribbon; on the ribbon was a cardboard medal; and on the medal a childish hand had scratched the legend, —

Miranda Terry.
If lost, please return her to her mother,
Angelina Terry,
87 Overlook Terrace.

It was such a card as Miss Terry herself had worn in the days when her mother had first let her and Tom go out on the street without a nurse.

Mary stared hard at the bit of cardboard. 87 Overlook Terrace! Yes, that was where she had found the doll. She remembered now seeing the name on a street corner. Miranda; what a pretty name for a doll! Angelina Terry; so that was the name of the little girl who had lost Miranda. Angelina must be feeling very sorry now. Perhaps she was crying herself to sleep, for it was growing late.

Her two girl cousins came romping into the bedroom. They had been having a hilarious evening.

"Hello, Mary!" they cried. "We heard about your great find!"—"Playing with your old doll, are you? Goin' to hang up her stockin' and see if Santa Claus will fill it?"—"Huh! Santa Claus won't come to this house, I guess!"

Mary had almost forgotten that it was Christmas Eve. There had been nothing in the house to remind her. Perhaps Angelina Terry had hung up a stocking for Miranda at 87 Overlook Terrace. But there would be no Miranda to see it the next morning.

Her cousins teased her for some time, while they undressed, and Mary grew sulky. She sat in her corner and answered them shortly. But presently the room was quiet, for the girls slept easily. Then Mary crept into her little cot with the doll in her arms. She loved Miranda so much that she would never part with her, no indeed; not even though she now knew where Miranda belonged. 87 Overlook Terrace! The figures danced before her eyes maliciously. She wished she could forget them. And the thought of Angelina Terry kept coming to her. Poor Angelina!

"She ain't 'poor Angelina,'" argued Mary to herself. "She's rich Angelina. Doesn't she live in a big house in the swell part of the city? I s'pose she has hundreds of dolls, much handsomer than Miranda, and lots of other toys. I guess she won't miss this one queer old doll. I guess she'd let me keep it if she knew I hadn't any of my own. I guess it ought to be my doll. Anyway, I'm going to keep her. I don't believe Angelina loves Miranda so much as I do."

She laid her cheek against the doll's cold waxen one and presently fell asleep.

But she slept uneasily. In the middle of the night she awoke and lay for hours tossing and unhappy in the stuffy little room. The clock struck one, two, three. At last she gave a great sigh, and cuddling Miranda in her arms turned over, with peace in her heart.

"I will play you are mine, my very own dollie, for just this one night," she whispered in Miranda's ear. "To-morrow will be Christmas Day, and I will take you back to your little mother, Angelina Terry. I can't do a mean thing at Christmas time,—not even for you, dear Miranda."

Thereupon she fell into a peaceful sleep.

CHAPTER XII
THE ANGEL AGAIN

"Will she bring it back?" asked Miss Terry eagerly, when once more she found herself under the gaze of the Christmas Angel. He nodded brightly.

"To-morrow morning you will see," he said. "It will prove that all I have shown you is really true."

"A pretty child," said Miss Terry musingly. "A very nice child indeed. I believe she looks very much as I used to be myself."

"You see, she is not a thief, after all; not yet," said the Angel. "What a pity that she must live in that sad home, with such terrible people! A sensitive child like her, craving sympathy and affection,—what chance has she for happiness? What would you yourself have been in surroundings like hers?"

"Yes, she is very like what I was. Of course I shall let her keep the doll."

Miss Terry hesitated. The Angel looked at her steadily and his glance seemed to read her half-formed thoughts.

"Surely," he said. "It seems to belong to her, does it not? But is this all? I wonder if something more does not belong to her."

"What more?" asked Miss Terry shortly.

"A home!" cried the Angel.

Miss Terry groped in her memory for a scornful ejaculation which she had once been fond of using, but there was no such word to be found. Instead there came to her lips the name, "Mary."

The Angel repeated it softly. "Mary. It is a blessed name," he said. "Blessed the roof that shelters a Mary in her need."

There was a long silence, in which Miss Terry felt new impulses stirring within her; impulses drawing her to the child whose looks recalled her own childhood. The Angel regarded her with beaming eyes. After some time he said quietly, "Now let us see what became of your last experiment."

Miss Terry started. It seemed as if she had been interrupted in pleasant dreaming. "You were the last experiment," she said. "I know what became of you. Here you are!"

"Yet more may have happened than you guessed," replied the Angel meaningly. "I have tried to show you how often that is the case. Look again."

Without moving from her chair Miss Terry seemed to be looking out on her sidewalk, where, so it seemed, she had just laid the pink figure of the Angel. She saw the drunken man approach. She heard his coarse laugh; saw his brutal movement as he kicked the Christmas token into the street. In sick disgust she saw him reel away out of sight. She saw herself run down the steps, rescue the image, and bring it into the house. Surely the story was finished. What more could there be?

But something bade her vision follow the steps of the wretched man. Down the street he reeled, singing a blasphemous song.

With a whoop he rounded a corner and ran into a happy party which filled sidewalk and street, as it hurried in the direction from which he came. Good-naturedly they jostled him against the wall, and he grasped a railing to steady himself as they swept by. It was the choir on their way to carol in the next street. Before them went the cross-bearer, lifting high his simple wooden emblem.

The eyes of the drunken man caught sight of this, and wavered. The presence of the crowd conveyed no meaning to his dazed brains. But there was something in the familiar symbol which held his vision. He looked, and crossed himself, remembering the traditions of his childhood. Some of the boys were humming as they went the stirring strains of an ancient Christmas march known to all nations; a carol which began, some say, as a rousing drinking chorus.

The familiar strain touched some chord in the sodden brain. The man gave a feeble whinny, trying to follow the melody. He pulled himself together and lurched forward in a sudden impulse to join the band of pilgrims. But by the time he had taken three steps they had vanished, miraculously, as it seemed to him.

"Begorra, they're gone!" he cried. "Who were they? Were they rale folks? What was it they was singin'?"

He sank back helplessly on a flight of steps. "Ve-ni-te a-do-re-mus!" he croaked in a quavering basso. And his tangled mind went through strange processes. Suddenly, there came to him in a flash of exaggerated memory the figure of the Christmas Angel which not ten minutes earlier he had kicked into the street. A pious horror fell upon him.

"Mither o' mercy!" he cried, again crossing himself. "What have I been an' done? It was a howly image; an' what did I do to ut? Lemme go back an' find ut, an' take ut up out av the street."

Greatly sobered by his fear, he staggered down the block and around the corner to the steps of Miss Terry's house.

"This is the place," he mused. "I know ut; here's where the frindly lam'post hild me in its arrums. I rimimber there was a dark house forninst me. Here's where ut lay on the sidewalk, all pink an' pretty. An' I kicked ut into the street! Where is ut now? Where gone? Howly Mither! Here's the spot where ut fell, look now! The shape of uts little body and the wings of ut in the snow. But 'tis gone intirely!" He rubbed his eyes and crossed himself again. "'Tis flown away," he muttered. "'Tis gone back to Hiven to tell Mary Mither o' the wicked thing I done this night. Oh, 'tis a miracle that's happened! An' oh! The wicked man I am, drunk and disorderly on the Howly Eve!" "O come, all ye faithful, Joyful and triumphant!"

Once more he heard the familiar strain taken up lustily by many voices.

"Hear all the world singin' on the way to Bethlehem!" he said, and the stupor seemed to leave his brain. He no longer staggered.

"I'll run an' join 'em, an' I won't drink another drop this night." He looked up at the starry sky. "Maybe the Angel hears me. Maybe he'll help me to keep straight to-morrow. It might be my Guardian Angel himsilf that I treated so! Saints forgive me!"

With head bowed humbly, but no longer reeling, he moved away towards the sound of music.

"You were his Guardian Angel," said Miss Terry, when once more she saw the figure on the mantel-shelf. And she spoke with reverent gentleness.

The Angel smiled brightly. "The Christmas Spirit is a guardian angel to many," he said. "Never again despise me, Angelina. Never again make light of my influence."

"Never again," murmured Miss Terry half unconsciously. "I wish it were not too late—"

"It is never too late," said the Christmas Angel eagerly, as if he read her unspoken thought. "Oh, never too late, Angelina."

CHAPTER XIII
THE CHRISTMAS CANDLE

Suddenly there was a sound,—a dull reverberating sound. It seemed to Miss Terry to come from neither north, south, east, nor west, but from a different world. Ah! She recognized it now. It was somebody knocking on the library door.

Miss Terry gave a long sigh and drew herself up in her chair. "It must be Norah just come back," she said to herself. "I had forgotten Norah completely. It must be shockingly late. Come in," she called, as she glanced at the clock.

She rubbed her eyes and looked again. A few minutes after nine! She had thought it must be midnight!

Norah entered to find her mistress staring at the mantel where the clock stood. She saw lying beside the clock the pink Angel which had fallen from the box as she brought it in,—the box now empty by the fire.

"Law, Miss," she said, "have you burned them all up but him? I'm glad you saved him, he's so pretty."

"Norah," said Miss Terry with an effort, "is that clock right?"

"Yes'm," said Norah. "I set it this morning. I came back as soon as I could, Miss," she added apologetically.

"It isn't that," answered Miss Terry, drawing her hand across her forehead dazedly. "I did not mind your absence. But I thought it must be later."

"Oh, no, I wouldn't stay out any later when you was alone here, Miss," said Norah penitently. "I felt ashamed after I had gone. I ought not to have left you so,—on Christmas Eve. But oh, Miss! The singing was so beautiful, and the houses looked so grand with the candles in the windows. It is like a holy night indeed!"

Miss Terry stooped and picked up something from the floor. It was the bit of candle-end which had escaped the holocaust.

"Are the candles still lighted, Norah?" she asked, eyeing the bit of wax in her hand.

"Yes'm, some of them," answered the maid. "It is getting late, and a good many have burned out. But some houses are still as bright as ever."

"Perhaps it is not too late, then," murmured Miss Terry, as if yielding a disputed point. "Let us hurry, Norah."

She rose, and going to the mantel-shelf gently took up the figure of the Angel, while Norah looked on in amazement.

"Norah," said Miss Terry, with an eagerness which made her voice tremble, "I want you to hang the Christmas Angel in the window there. I too have a fancy to burn a candle to-night. If it is not too late I'd like to have a little share in the Christmas spirit."

Norah's eyes lighted. "Oh, yes'm," she said. "I'll hang it right away. And I'll find an empty spool to hold the candle."

She bustled briskly about, and presently in the window appeared a little device unlike any other in the block. Against the darkness within, the figure of the Angel with arms outstretched towards the street shone in a soft light from the flame of a single tiny candle such as blossom on Christmas trees.

It caught the attention of many home-goers, who said, smiling, "How simple! How pretty! How quaint! It is a type of the Christmas spirit which is abroad to-night. You can feel it everywhere, blessing the city."

For some minutes before the candle was lighted, a man muffled in a heavy overcoat had been standing in a doorway opposite Miss Terry's house. He was tall and grizzled and his face was sad. He stared up at the gloomy windows, the only oblongs of blackness in the illuminated block, and he shivered, shrugging his shoulders.

"The same as ever!" he said to himself. "I might have known she would never change. Any one else, on Christmas Eve, after the letter I wrote her, would have softened a little. But I might have known. She is hard as nails! Of course, it was my fault in the first place to leave her as I did. But when I acknowledged it, and when I wrote that letter on Christmas Eve, I thought Angelina might feel differently." He looked at his watch. "Nearly half-past nine," he muttered. "I may as well go home. She said she wanted to be let alone; that Christmas meant nothing to her. I don't dare to call,—on my only sister! I suppose she is there all alone, and here I am all alone, too. What a pity! If I saw the least sign—"

Just then there was the spark of a match against the darkness framed in by the window opposite. A hand and arm shone in the flicker of light across the upper sash. A tiny spark, tremulous at first, like a bird alighting on a frail branch, paused, steadied, and became fixed. In the light of a small taper the man caught a glimpse of a pale, long face in a frame of silver hair. It faded into the background. But above the candle he now saw, with arms outstretched as it seemed toward himself, a pink little angel with gauzy wings.

The man's heart gave a leap. Sudden memories thronged his brain, making him almost dizzy. At last they formulated into one smothered cry. "The Christmas Angel! It is the very same pink Angel that Angelina and I used to hang on our Christmas tree!"

In three great leaps, like a schoolboy, he crossed the street and ran up the steps of Number 87. The Christmas Angel seemed to smile with ineffable sweetness as he gave the bell a vigorous pull.

CHAPTER XIV
TOM

Miss Terry was leaning on the mantel-shelf looking into the fire, when the bell pealed furiously. She started and turned pale.

"Lord 'a' mercy!" ejaculated Norah, who was still admiring the effect of the window-decoration. "What's that? Who can be calling here to-night, making such a noise?"

"Go to the door, Norah," said Miss Terry with a strange note in her voice. "It may be some one to see me. It is not too late."

"Yes'm," said Norah, obedient but bewildered.

Presently the library door opened and a figure strode in; a tall, broad-shouldered man in a fur overcoat. For a moment he stood just inside the door, hesitating. Miss Terry took two steps forward from the fire-place.

"Tom!" she said faintly. "You came,—after all!"

"After all, Angelina," he said. "Yes, because I saw that," he waved his hand toward the window. "That gave me courage to come in. It is our Christmas Angel. I remember all about it. Does it mean anything, Angelina?"

Miss Terry held out a moment longer. Then she faltered forward. "O Tom!" she sobbed, as she felt his brotherly, strong arms about her. "O Tom! And so he has brought you back to me, and me to you!"

"He? Angelina girl, who?" He smoothed her silver hair with rough, kind fingers.

"Why, the Christmas Angel; our Guardian Angel, Tom. All these years I kept him in the play box, and I was going to burn him up. But I couldn't do it, Tom. How wonderful it is!"

They sat down before the fire and she began to tell him the whole story. But she interrupted herself to send for Norah, who came to her, mystified and half scandalized by the greeting which she had seen those two oldsters exchange.

"This is my brother Tom, Norah, who has come back," she said. "I believe it is not too late to make some preparation for Christmas Day. The stores will still be open. Run out and order things for a grand occasion, Norah. And—O Norah!" a sudden remembrance came to her. "If you have time, will you please get some toys and pretty things such as a little girl would like; a little girl of about ten, with my complexion,—I mean, with yellow hair and blue eyes. We may have a little guest to-morrow."

"Yes'm," said Norah, moving like one in a dream.

"A guest?" exclaimed Tom. And Miss Terry told him about Mary.

"I love little girls," said Tom, "especially little girls with yellow hair and blue eyes, such as you used to have, Angelina."

"You will like Mary, then," said Miss Terry, with a pretty pink flush of pleasure in her cheeks.

"I shall like her, if she comes," amended Tom, who, man-like, received with reservations the account of a vision vouchsafed not unto him.

"She will come," said Miss Terry with her old positiveness, glancing towards the window where the Christmas Angel hung.

Then arose the sound of singing outside the house. The passing choristers had spied the quaint window, now the only one in the street which remained lighted:—

"When Christ was born of Mary free, In Bethlehem, in that fair citye, Angels sang with mirth and glee, In Excelsis Gloria!"

And Mary came. The brother and sister were at breakfast,—the happiest which either of them had known for years,—when there came a timid pull at the front-door bell. Miss Angelina laid down her knife and fork and looked across the table at Tom.

"She has come. Mary has come," she said. "Norah, if it is a little girl with a package under her arm, bring her in here."

"Yes'm!" gasped Norah, who believed she was living in a dream where everything was topsy-turvy. When had a child entered Miss Terry's dining-room!

Norah disappeared and presently returned ushering in a little girl of ten, with blue eyes and yellow hair. Under her arm she carried a white-paper package, very badly wrapped.

Miss Terry exchanged with her brother a glance which said, "I told you so!"
The child seemed bashful and afraid to speak; no wonder!

Tom's kind heart yearned to her. "Good morning! Wish you a merry Christmas, Mary!" he said smiling.

The child gave a start. "Why, how did you know my name?" she cried.

Tom looked confused. How indeed did he know? But Miss Angelina, with a readiness that surprised herself, came to his rescue.

"We were talking of a little girl named Mary," she said. "And you look just like her. What did you come for, dear?"

The little girl hung her head and turned crimson.

"I—I came to see Angelina Terry," she whispered. "I—I've got a doll that belongs to her."

There was a pause, then Miss Terry said, "Well, go on."

"I—I found her on the steps of this house last night, and I ought to have brought her right here then. But I didn't. I took her home. I hope Angelina was not very unhappy last night." Miss Terry smiled upon Tom, who gave a kind, low laugh.

"No," said Miss Terry. "Angelina did not worry about her lost doll. She was thinking about something else,—the nicest Christmas present that ever anybody had. But you were a good girl to bring back the doll."

"No, I'm not a good girl," said Mary, and her voice trembled. "I was a wicked girl. I meant to keep Miranda for myself, because I thought she would be a lovely big doll. And when I found she was old and homely, somehow I still wanted to keep her. But it was stealing, and I couldn't. Please, will you give her to Angelina, and tell her I am so sorry?" She took Miranda out of the wrapping and held her toward Miss Terry without looking at the doll. It was as if she were afraid of being tempted once more.

Miss Terry did not take the doll.

"I am Angelina," she said. "The doll was mine."

"You! Angelina!" the child's face was full of bewilderment. Mechanically she drew Miranda to her and clasped her close.

"Yes, I am Angelina, and that was my doll Miranda," said Miss Terry gently. "Thank you for returning her. But Mary,—your name is Mary?" The child nodded.—"Suppose I wanted you to keep her for me, what would you say?"

Mary's eyes still dwelt upon Miss Terry with a puzzled look. This gray-haired Angelina was so different from the one she had pictured. She did not answer the question. Miss Terry drew the child to a chair beside her.

"Tell me all about yourself, Mary," she said.

After some coaxing and prompting from what they already guessed, Mary told the story of her sad little life.

She was an orphan recently left to the care of her uncle and aunt, who had received her grudgingly. They were her sole relatives; and the shame of their degraded lives was plain through the outlines of the vague picture which Mary sketched of them.

"You do not love them, Mary?" asked Miss Terry kindly.

"No," answered the child. "They always speak crossly to me. When they have been drinking they beat me."
Tom rose from the table with a muttered word and began to pace the floor. His blue eyes were full of tears.

"Mary," said Miss Terry, "will the people at home be worried if you do not come back to dinner?"

Mary shook her head wonderingly. "No," she said. "They will not care. I am often away on holidays. I go to the Museums."

"Then I want you to stay with us to-day," said Miss Terry. "We are going to have a Christmas celebration, and we need you for a guest. Will you stay, you and Miranda?"

Mary looked down at the doll in her arms, and up at the two kind faces bent toward her. "Yes," she said impulsively, "I will stay. How good you are! I don't want to go home."

"Don't go home!" burst out Tom. "Stay with us always and be our little girl."

Mary looked from one to the other, half frightened at the new idea. Miss Terry bent and pecked at her cheek, with a thrill at the new sensation.

"Yes, we mean it," she said, and her voice was almost sweet. "We believe that the Christmas Angel has brought you to us, Mary. You have the Christmas name. But you seem to us like the little girl we both knew best, little Angelina with blue eyes and yellow hair, who was Miranda's mother. Will you stay with us, Mary Angelina? Would you like to stay?"

Mary looked up with a wistful smile. "You are so good!" she said again. "I wish I could stay. But Uncle and Aunt are so—I am afraid of what they might do to us all. If they thought you wanted me, they would not let me go."

"I will fix Uncle and Aunt," said Tom, going for his coat. "Leave them to me. I know an argument that settles uncles and aunts of that sort. You need not go back to their house, I promise you, Mary, my dear."

Mary gave a great sigh of relief. "Oh, I am so glad!" she said. "It was such a wicked house. And here it is so good!"

"Good!" Miss Terry echoed the word with a sigh. "Come with me, Mary," she said.

She led her little guest through the hall to the library, where a great fire was blazing, with sundry mysterious packages in white paper piled on the table beside it. But Miss Terry did not stop at the fire-place. She drew Mary to the window which looked out on the sidewalk. Above the lower sash Mary saw the remains of a burned-out Christmas candle; and over it hung a pink papier-mâché Angel stretching out open arms towards her.

"This is the Christmas Angel, Mary," said Miss Terry. "He is as old as Miranda—"

"He is as old as Christmas," interrupted Tom, looking in from the hall.

"When we were children, Tom and I, we hung him on our Christmas tree," went on Miss Terry. "We think he brought you to us. We believe he has changed the world for us,—has brought us peace, good-will, and happiness. He is going to be the guardian angel of our house. You must love him, Mary."

"How beautiful he is!" said Mary reverently. "His face shines like the Baby's that I saw once in the Church. Oh, Miss Angelina! He is like the Christ-Child himself!"

"Call me Aunt Angelina," said Miss Terry with a quick breath.

"Aunt Angelina," cried the child, throwing her arms about Miss Terry's neck.

Tom came and put his great furry coat-sleeves about them both. "And Uncle Tom," he said.

"Dear Uncle Tom!" whispered the child shyly.

There were tears in the eyes of all three.

"Now we shall live happy ever after," said Tom.

And the Christmas Angel beamed upon them.